CHANGING PLACES

Written by Nette Hilton
Illustrated by Lucia Masciullo

Published by Pearson Education Limited, Edinburgh Gate, Harlow, Essex, CM20 2JE
Registered company number: 872828

www.pearsonschools.co.uk

Designed by Bigtop

Illustrated by Lucia Masciullo

First published 2012

23
13

British Library Cataloguing in Publication Data
A catalogue record for this book is available from the British Library

ISBN 978 0 435 07581 1

Printed and bound in Great Britain by Bell & Bain Ltd, Glasgow.

Acknowledgements
We would like to thank the children and teachers of Bangor Central Integrated Primary School, NI; Bishop Henderson C of E Primary School, Somerset; Brookside Community Primary School, Somerset; Cheddington Combined School, Buckinghamshire; Cofton Primary School, Birmingham; Dair House Independent School, Buckinghamshire; Deal Parochial School, Kent; Holy Trinity Catholic Primary School, Chipping Norton; Lawthorn Primary School, North Ayrshire; Newbold Riverside Primary School, Rugby and Windmill Primary School, Oxford for their invaluable help in the development and trialling of the Bug Club resources.

Contents

CHAPTER ONE
Oska

Thursday was the worst day of my life. It should have been one of the best because, in two days' time, Oska Binns was going to come with me to the zoo.

By Thursday I was so excited that I couldn't stop grinning. Oska was grinning too, but he was REALLY excited.

"Guess what?" he said.

"What?"

"We're moving house."

I didn't think that was a good idea. Oska had lived next door forever. But when I looked over the fence I saw some big boxes lined up, and his mum and dad starting to take them into the house to sort things into them.

"When?" I said.

"Soon," said Oska.

We sat on the step. It's hard to feel good about a zoo when you feel bad about a friend.

"How about sorting out all those stamps that you've collected?" Mum said. "It might make you feel better."

"Cool," said Oska.

I wondered if Oska felt sad, too.

We looked at the stamps, muddled together in a big, old shoe box.

"Let's put all the animal stamps in a stack over here," Oska said. So we did. Then we put the car stamps together, but Oska said a Jaguar is a car *and* an animal – so we had to start all over again.

“Let’s make a zoo scrapbook,” I said.

“Cool,” said Oska.

I got some paper and we started to make the scrapbook. Oska stuck a car stamp right in the middle. “It’s a Jaguar!” he laughed.

I drew some bars and a cage around it. We were so busy laughing that I forgot about Oska moving house.

For a little while.

CHAPTER TWO

Laughter and Sadness

When the scrapbook we were making stopped being fun, we went and sat in the sun.

"When are you going?" I asked again.

"Soon."

"How soon?"

"I'm not sure," Oska said. "But we're going to the zoo first! Cool!"

Itchi slumped down beside us on the step.

"She looks like a lion, stretched out like that!" Oska said.

Itchi took off, and we chased her all around the back garden and through a left-over muddy puddle to catch her.

"This lion needs a bath," Oska said.

Itchi heard. She raced away again as fast as she could.

"I don't think lions like having baths," I said.

"You catch her, and I'll get the hose!" Oska yelled. He waited until Itchi and I

were beside him, then he squirted me. Itchi barked and I yelped, but we soon got busy. Oska did Itchi's head and I got the bottom end, and we all finished up soaked and soapy. Then Itchi shook herself and raced inside to roll on the carpet and ... right through the stacks of stamps.

We howled with laughter.

"At least she'll get posted back if she gets lost," Oska said.

Then, suddenly, I felt sad all over again.

"Can *people* get posted back, do you think?"

Oska looked at me.

Maybe sadness is like measles because it looked, right then, as if Oska might have caught mine.

"You're mad," he said, and we laughed about people getting stuck in the post box. I laughed louder than Oska, because I didn't want him to catch any more of my sadness.

It didn't seem fair.

CHAPTER THREE

Holding on Tight

On Saturday, we got up early and drove across the city to the zoo.

It was brilliant.

We saw monkeys and penguins and meerkats.

"Cool!" Oska said.

We saw a log that had a wildcat inside, but we didn't see the wildcat. We saw snakes sleeping with their eyes open. Something tickled my leg and I shrieked.

I was sure it was a great, big, fat python, but it was only Oska playing a joke.

I chased him all the way down the hill to the ostrich enclosure. There was an ostrich standing head down and rear up. Oska laughed so loud that the ostrich swooshed dust all over him.

It was so funny, I forgot about Oska moving house and being sad. I think Oska did, too. And when we climbed up to the bears and helped feed carrots to the giraffes and raced fast down the long, steep hill, we didn't have time to be sad.

We were too busy being best friends.

And holding on tight to that.

CHAPTER FOUR
Pink and Red Flowers

Last week, Oska Binns left.

The furniture van drove away and Oska's car followed like a sad little duckling not sure of the way.

I watched it leave.

"You'll feel better in a little while," Dad reckoned.

How could I? Oska's house was so empty it had tummy rumbles. Soon, the grass started growing longer and Oska's tyre swing got rain-spotted and dusty.

Itchi took me walking around Oska's back garden. We used to run around here, but now Itchi was getting so fat she could hardly waddle.

Nobody seemed to care about Oska's house.

"Ew," they said. "It needs some paint."

"Too many trees," they said. "And that swing is falling down."

"Pity no one cares about this house any more," they said.

I cared about it.

I got a bucket and washed the old swing. It looked black and shiny again. I borrowed the broom and swept the footpath. I dug in the garden and took out some of the weeds.

Itchi helped. She'd got so fat she didn't dig for long, though. Mostly, she just crept around looking for places to sleep.

"Even Itchi's sad," I said.

Mum smiled. "Itchi'll be all right. She's not her usual self, though, so you'll have to keep an eye on her."

Mum gave me some plants with pink and red flowers. "These will cheer the place up a bit."

Dad even mowed the grass.

By the time I had dug some holes and the new plants were uncurling their roots like toes wriggling into a new pair of slippers, the sun was making long shadows across the grass.

And I had forgotten about Itchi.

CHAPTER FIVE
Night Sounds

"Where's Itchi gone?" I said. "She's always here at bedtime."

I called and called but she didn't come waddling up the hall like she usually did.

"She won't be far," Mum said.

But she might be.

I tried to think about the places she liked to go. And I tried *not* to think about the roads and the big, fast lorries that raced along them at night.

Or perhaps someone had seen her and thought, "What a funny, fat dog. I'll give her a lift," and took her a long way away.

I should have watched out for her.

I crept out of my bed and looked out of the window at Oska Binns' house. The moonlight picked out the flowers and made a silvery shine on the old swing.

"Itchi!" I called into the night. "Where are you?"

Oska Binns' house didn't stir. The moon winked across the windows, and, for a moment, I thought I saw Oska's face grinning out at me the way it used to.

"I can't find Itchi," I whispered.

But Oska was gone.

And so was Itchi.

Great, fat tears rolled down my face. I leaned my head against the window and I thought I saw the swing swaying happily in the moonlight.

And I thought I heard something, too. It sounded like Oska laughing the way he used to when the swing twirled too hard.

"It's not funny!" I cried.

"What's not funny?" Mum switched on the light.

I told her about the noise and she listened to all the night sounds. Then she smiled.

"Come with me," she said.

CHAPTER SIX
Itchi's Surprise

Together, we crept out of the house. The moon shone down on us as we climbed over the fence and into Oska's garden.

The swing twisted happily.

"Has Oska come home?" I said.

Perhaps Oska knew that Itchi had gone missing, and had come back to make me feel better.

Mum stopped. She bent down and gave me a big hug. "No," she said. "But I think Itchi has. Listen carefully."

I heard it again. Soft, high sounds that weren't laughing at all.

We crept round the back of the house. The sounds were sharper here. I heard the soft rumble that Itchi makes.

"What are you doing here, girl?" I said. "Are you hurt?"

Mum shone the torch down.

Itchi grinned up at me.

I grinned back.

"She wasn't just fat, was she?" I said, as we loaded six sleepy puppies into our laps.

I looked at Oska Binns' house and felt the warm bulge of new puppies in my hands.

I smiled at Oska's house. "It's looking better," I thought, "even in moonlight. And tomorrow, it'll be better still."

CHAPTER SEVEN
Mitzi

Even with the new puppies the days still dragged by, as saggy as a trampoline that had forgotten how to bounce. I didn't think I was going to have a springy time ever again. I'd just about given up, when one day I woke up and knew something was going to happen.

The puppies were tumbling and trying to be tough, barking like they always did in the mornings. I was used to getting up and taking care not to step on one. Or on anything else that they'd left behind.

So it wasn't the puppies that were different. It was something else that made me feel excited. There was a birthday hum in my head and it wasn't my birthday.

I looked out at Oska Binns' house. The flowers nodded as if they knew something.

But I didn't.

The swing swung itself in the sort of circle that made me sick if I were riding on it.

But I wasn't.

"What's up?" I said, checking to see if perhaps Christmas had come and I'd forgotten. Mum was grinning. So was Dad.

"Have a look out the front," they said.

There was the biggest, reddest lorry I'd ever seen. All sorts of cartons and boxes were lolling about on the pavement.

I went outside.

"Hey! What are you doing outside in your pyjamas?" a loud voice cried.

A football, and then a girl, landed on my side of the fence.

"You'd better say hello, then," she said, and booted the ball my way.

"Hello," I said, and ducked.

"My name's Mitzi Mickleham and I live in that house, next door!"

"You can't," I said. "That's Oska Binns' house!"

"Yeah, well ..." The girl looked over the fence. "He's not using it any more, is he?"

I kicked her ball back over the fence.

"You could use some lessons," she said, as she jumped back into Oska's garden. "You're not such a good footy player, are you?"

"And I'll bet you wouldn't know what a stamp collection was!" I yelled. "Or how to make a scrapbook!"

I don't know if she heard me or not, but she didn't come back.

Itchi stood by the fence in case she did. Her puppies rolled around like footballs.

CHAPTER EIGHT

Two Best Friends

It'd serve her right, that Mitzi Mickleham, if I called her and her ball back. I could let her try to teach me to play football.

And she'd learn that she's not welcome in Oska Binns' house.

And Itchi would have a brand new ball in her back-of-the-shed collection. Itchi liked balls. Any balls.

I called Mitzi. I yelled in my loudest voice and she yelled back.

Her voice was even louder. “I’m on my way, Spike!”

My name isn’t Spike, it’s Max, but I went and got dressed anyway. By the time I found my football-kicking shoes,

Mitzi Mickleham was already at my back door. She was wearing really-trulio football boots.

I looked at my school shoes.

“They’ll do for a little bit,” Mitzi said.

She gave the ball a great, hard kick. The ball flew into the air like it was in a hurry to get out of the way.

Mitzi flew after it.

So did Itchi.

I ran a little bit, but not very much.

"Run faster!" Mitzi ordered, and kicked the ball again. "Brilliant!" she cried as Itchi leaped up to try to catch the ball. "Go Becks!"

"Her name is Itchi!" I shouted.

Mitzi wasn't listening. She'd kicked the ball again and Itchi flew into the air to try and stop it.

I got beside Itchi.

"No, Spike!" yelled Mitzi. "Get in front of her!"

I tried, but I wasn't fast enough. And it was hard jumping lots of excited puppies.

Itchi got the ball. She hit it with her nose and it flew across the garden. She pounced on it and it flew into the wet grass. She rolled on it, and it landed in Dad's vegetable patch.

Which had manure on it.

So did Itchi.

I didn't care. I raced after her and kicked the ball. I kicked it hard enough to send some of my Oska-sadness sailing away with it.

It must have worked because I started to laugh. "You're pretty good at this!" Mitzi said as I leaped over the fence and kicked the ball back.

"Go Spike!" she said.

We kicked that ball and chased it until we were so tired we had to flop onto our backs on the lawn. Itchi flopped too.

"PHEEEEEEW!" Mitzi said. "That dog really pongs!"

Suddenly, I had an excellent idea.

"Do you want to help me bath her?"

"Brilliant!" Mitzi said.

I got the hose and she got Itchi. I waited until they came round the corner. Mitzi really yelled when I turned on the hose. The water splashed all over her and she laughed and laughed. Then she chased me and splashed me. We both laughed so hard our sides ached.

"Cool," I said.

It really was.

It was so cool, I wrote to Oska and told him all about it.

I told him you can't post people or dogs through the mail, ha, ha, ha. But I could post him jokes and news about Mitzi Mickleham and football.

And just because I have a new friend, it doesn't mean that he isn't still my best friend.

It's just that now, I've got two of them.